W9-ALM-487

PHILOSOPHERS OF
THE ENLIGHTENMENT™

JEAN-JACQUES
ROUSSEAU

Advocate of
Government
by Consent

PHILOSOPHERS OF
THE ENLIGHTENMENT™

JEAN-JACQUES ROUSSEAU

Advocate of Government by Consent

James R. Norton

The Rosen Publishing Group, Inc., New York

J100
NOR

To my parents

Published in 2006 by The Rosen Publishing Group, Inc.
29 East 21st Street, New York, NY 10010

Copyright © 2006 by The Rosen Publishing Group, Inc.

First Edition

All rights reserved. No part of this book may be reproduced in any form without permission in writing from the publisher, except by a reviewer.

Library of Congress Cataloging-in-Publication Data

Norton, James R.
Jean-Jacques Rousseau: advocate of government by consent/by James R. Norton.—1st ed.
    p. cm.—(Philosophers of the Enlightenment)
Includes bibliographical references and index.
ISBN 1-4042-0422-9 (library binding: alk. paper)
1. Rousseau, Jean-Jacques, 1712–1778.
I. Title. II. Series.
B2137.N67 2005
194—dc22

2004030623

Manufactured in Malaysia

On the cover: Head-and-shoulder portrait of Jean-Jacques Rousseau *(foreground)*; *Taking of the Bastille, July 14, 1789*, an eighteenth-century painting portraying one of the most dramatic events of the French Revolution.

CONTENTS

Introduction 7

CHAPTER 1   A Boy from Geneva 10

CHAPTER 2   Paris and the *Encyclopedia* 22

CHAPTER 3   Two Discourses 31

CHAPTER 4   *The Social Contract* and *Émile* 51

CHAPTER 5   Words of Revolution 78

Timeline 97

Glossary 99

For More Information 103

For Further Reading 105

Bibliography 106

Index 108

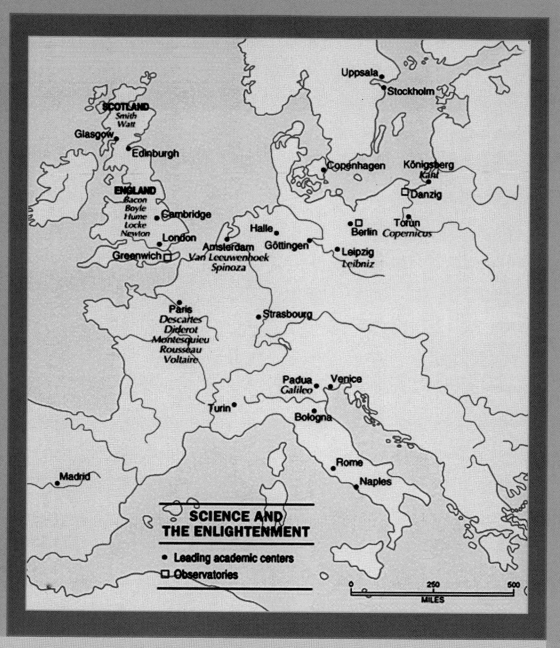

Paris was the intellectual center of the Enlightenment. However, the revolutionary scientific and philosophical ideas of the era sprang up in various places across western Europe. This map shows the leading academic centers and scientific observatories in Europe during the Enlightenment.

INTRODUCTION

"Man was born free, and he is everywhere in chains."

When Jean-Jacques Rousseau wrote these words in 1762, slavery was a thriving international business. Kings and queens ruled with limitless power, and in Europe, the Catholic Church was a political powerhouse that used its wealth and power to determine the fate of nations. In Rousseau's time, it was never taken for granted that all people, including the poorest and weakest, had the right to freedom and a personal stake in government.

Rousseau was born in Geneva, Switzerland, in 1712; a week later, his mother died. His father, Isaac, a watchmaker, raised Rousseau, cultivating his son's love of books and learning. At fifteen years old, Rousseau left his hometown. He traveled throughout

This nineteenth-century portrait of Jean-Jacques Rousseau by Edward Lacretelle shows the philosopher as a young man, perhaps around the time he was beginning to establish himself as a serious thinker. Arguably the most influential of the Enlightenment philosophers, Rousseau was a creative writer whose passionate explanations of his philosophy made him a lot of enemies, even among other writers who could have been natural allies.

Europe before settling down with a Swiss baroness, Madame Françoise-Louise de Warens, who would become his teacher and, eventually, his lover.

"Until he was well into his thirties," the historian Paul Johnson writes in his book *Intellectuals*, "Rousseau led a life of failure and dependence, especially on women. He tried at least thirteen jobs, as an engraver, lackey . . . and private secretary."

Not much about this bearish man, described by friends as "lovably simple," suggested the influence he would have in later years. His ideas redefined the way school is taught and the way children learn. They fed the raging argument in the eighteenth century over the meaning of "freedom." They challenged the understanding that people serve their rulers, suggesting that the only true rulers are the people themselves. And they fueled the influential and violent French Revolution of 1789.

Over the course of his life, Rousseau would be celebrated by philosophers and the king of France, be driven from his home by a stone-throwing mob, be denounced by former friends, and see his books burned in the streets of his hometown. Despite all the challenges he faced, he left an indelible mark on history.

His story begins in the mountains of modern-day Switzerland.

A BOY FROM GENEVA

Some people escape their hometowns, shake the dust from their shoes, and never look back. Others never leave. Still others, like Rousseau, tour the world but remain deeply attached to the place where they grew up.

During Rousseau's lifetime, Geneva was a small, largely Protestant country in the mountains, not yet part of the nation we now know as Switzerland. Surrounded by gorgeous natural scenery, including Lake Geneva, the independent city was filled with craftsmen who had some—but not a lot of—money, relative to Europeans in general. It also had a keen interest in education.

Geneva was a republic, meaning that its citizens elected their leaders, who ruled in their name. Many of Rousseau's later ideas about

Although a haven for Protestants running away from religious intolerance in other countries, Geneva had its share of political and economic inequalities. Only a tiny fraction of its inhabitants were citizens. The government was dominated by a few major wealthy families who segregated themselves in one section of the city. This engraving offers a view of Geneva in the eighteenth century.

government would be inspired by memories of his birthplace.

Rousseau and his family had long, complicated ties to Geneva. His grandfather David Rousseau was a follower of a politician named Pierre Fatio. In 1707, the Genevan authorities executed Fatio, who was a champion of the city's craftsmen against its richest and most powerful citizens.

Rousseau was born five years later. His mother's death, so soon after his birth, left him living with his father in Geneva. In his "Letter to M. D'Alembert on the Theater" (written when he was forty-five), he provides a glimpse of his early years:

> I remember being struck in my childhood by a rather simple scene . . . the St. Gervais militia had completed their exercises and, as was the custom, each of the companies ate together; and after supper most of them met in the square of St. Gervais, where the officers and soldiers all danced together around the fountain.
>
> My father, embracing me, was thrilled in a way that I can still feel and share. "Jean-Jacques," he said to me, "love your country. Look at these good Genevans; they are friends. They are all brothers; joy and harmony reigns among them. You are a Genevan. One day you will see other nations, but even if you travel as far as your father has, you will never find any people to match your own."

In addition to teaching Rousseau a sense of Genevan patriotism, his father taught him the writings of the Roman historian Plutarch. The famous patriotism of Romans under their republic was one of Rousseau's great inspirations when he crafted his idea for how to design a fair and truly democratic government.

His father was expelled from Geneva in 1722 because he challenged a person of higher rank than himself to a duel. This taught Rousseau a hard early lesson in the inequality of the classes. Rousseau stayed in the city with relatives for a few more years.

Plutarch ranks among the most important of the ancient philosophers. He was born and lived in first-century Greece, but he traveled extensively throughout the then-known world. His biographies on Greek and Roman leaders, as well as his essays on morality, have had a significant influence on English and French literature.

In *The Confessions* (Les Confessions), Rousseau wrote about his early days in Geneva, recalling time spent with a favorite cousin:

We constructed cages, pipes, kites, drums, and model houses, toy guns and bows and blunted my poor old grandfather's tools,

LES
CONFESSIONS
DE
J. J. ROUSSEAU.

LIVRE PREMIER.

JE forme une entreprise qui n'eut jamais d'exemple, & dont l'exécution n'aura point d'imitateur. Je veux montrer à mes semblables un homme dans toute la vérité de la nature ; & cet homme, ce sera moi.

Tome I.   A

Rousseau wrote *The Confessions* toward the end of his life. Written between 1765 and 1775, but published after his death, it is an autobiography in which he justifies himself against his critics. It is widely considered one of his greatest works. A page from an early printing of the book is pictured here.

imitating him in the craft of watchmaking. But our especial preference was for scribbling on paper, drawing, color washing, painting, and generally wasting the materials.

Though his early years in Geneva and elsewhere were marked by long lazy periods, failure, and frustration, the city's mark would influence many of his latter works, including *The Social Contract* (Du Contrat Social; 1762), one of his most important books.

GENEVA'S GOVERNMENT

Unlike many other European states, which were ruled by monarchs, Geneva was run by a system of people's councils. There was a General Council, which was made up of all voting citizens. It had no debates. Instead, it silently voted on proposals that came from two smaller councils. This meant that although ordinary citizens couldn't suggest new laws, they had a right to approve or reject laws and proposals that the state of Geneva was considering.

The first of the smaller councils, the Council of Two Hundred, debated policies to submit to the General Council and acted as the city's supreme court of justice. This meant that it listened to difficult court cases that had been appealed from the lower courts and made a final decision in favor of the plaintiff or defendant. In addition to these duties, it elected the Council of Twenty-five, which was the smallest—and in some ways the most powerful— council. The Council of Twenty-five judged all criminal cases, nominated public servants, and set the city's budget. Its members served for life, so they had a great deal of long-term power over the city's government.

Unlike many other European states at the time, Geneva was able to provide many benefits to its citizens in return for their taxes. Because Geneva enjoyed a healthy trade with other states and many of its citizens were skilled laborers, the state was able to provide decent education and affordable food. In short, by any standard, Geneva was a great place to live, and its republican government was part of its appeal to thinkers like Rousseau. About Geneva he would later write, in a letter to a friend living there:

> All the circumstances of my life have served to give more fire to that ardent love of country which my father inspired in me. It is as a result of living (in exile) among slaves that I

have come to feel the value of liberty. How happy are you to dwell among men who obey only the laws, that is to say, Reason.

He would later change his mind about his hometown, but not before it helped inspire *The Social Contract*.

Despite the city's relative stability and his sometimes carefree upbringing, Rousseau left Geneva in 1728, when he began a series of travels that would take him to Italy, France, and other parts of Switzerland.

MADAME DE WARENS

In 1731, young Rousseau settled down in Chambéry, France, with a wealthy young widow, Madame de Warens. In the course of his travels, he had converted to Roman Catholicism, which eased his entry into the world of the Catholic Warens.

Rousseau's long stay in Chambéry was critical to his development, as he had long tumbled from place to place and from job to job. Warens, who was in some ways the great love of Rousseau's life, supported him while he educated himself, reading books from her extensive library.

Many young writers, scientists, and artists of the eighteenth century received financial backing and introductions to influential people from wealthy women, with whom they often had romantic relationships. Madame Françoise-Louise de Warens (*right*) was Rousseau's patron and lover for many years. Pictured above is Rousseau's bedroom at her country estate in Chambery.

While staying with Warens, Rousseau studied music, which would be critical for his later establishment as a thinker and semicelebrity in Paris. More important, he read the works of philosophers including Thomas Hobbes, John Locke, Samuel von Pufendorf, and Jean-Jacques Burlamaqui. Although he would later attack many of the ideas of these men, their writings served as an essential framework for Rousseau's thought.

VENICE AND BEYOND

Rousseau's stay in Chambéry eventually came to end in 1738, when an illness forced him to travel to Montpellier, France, in search of treatment. In the meantime, both he and Warens found new romantic partners, and their relationship changed. He was no longer welcome in Chambéry.

Rousseau was adrift again. He taught for a short while in France, in 1740, giving it up after discovering that he wasn't very good at teaching, and that he didn't enjoy it.

He then went to Paris, where he presented a new kind of musical notation to the Academy of Sciences. It failed, having been declared neither original nor particularly good.

A seeming stroke of luck occurred in Paris in 1742. The ambassador to Venice, Count Pierre François de Montagu, hired Rousseau to be his personal secretary. Rousseau was off to Venice, Italy, the city of canals and gondolas (small boats that act as taxis between Venice's many little islands).

The relationship with his new boss was a disaster. Rousseau, who was as arrogant as he was brilliant, made himself unpopular in many ways. He would, for example, borrow the ambassador's gondola without permission. Also, when the ambassador was trying to dictate to him and struggling to find a particular word, Rousseau would yawn out of obvious boredom or gaze out the window rather than listen to his boss.

In turn, he felt used by the ambassador and that he was treated like a servant although he was using his considerable talents to assist his boss in the complicated art of diplomacy.

Rousseau's stay in Venice ended poorly. He skipped town to avoid arrest after his enraged employer petitioned the Venetian Senate to have Rousseau imprisoned for vague charges of wrongdoing. Though he managed to stay out of prison, he also failed to collect his paycheck for a year's work.

However, his time in the city of canals was not entirely wasted. While in Venice, Rousseau learned its system of government, which he would later denounce as a corrupting influence on its people. His experience there provided an inspiration to come up with a more pure and honest way that people might be governed, and a challenge to figure out a system of government that was honest and legitimate.

PARIS AND THE ENCYCLOPEDIA

In 1745, Rousseau returned to Paris after his disgraceful exit from Venice. Few could have guessed that he would soon become one of the most famous men in the world of French literature. After years of struggle and failure, he was on the brink of bringing together his young life experience into his first major musical and philosophical works.

Soon after arriving in Paris, Rousseau began contributing to an ambitious new project known as the *Encyclopedia* (Encyclopédie). This collection of articles was originally intended to be a translation of an English work that collected various articles about topics in the arts and sciences. However, the translation's editors, Denis Diderot and Jean Le Rond d'Alembert, had a much bigger project in mind. As ambitious philosophers, they weren't content to merely translate the British book from English into French. Instead, they assembled some of France's leading minds to write a collection of new articles that were on the cutting edge of Enlightenment thinking.

The Enlightenment was an informal movement of eighteenth-century philosophers who shared a distrust of the ideas of the established, traditional Christian church. For example, traditional Catholic teachings suggested that priests—and the church— could help attract God's blessings for their parishioners. These teachings were also used to raise a great deal of money and support from church followers, making the church into a powerful political force. Enlightenment thinkers often not only rejected the priest as an unnecessary obstacle between man and God, but they also sometimes questioned or rejected the existence of God in the first place.

Many of its leading thinkers (including Diderot and Voltaire, another major contributor to the *Encyclopedia*) also believed in humanity's overall progress through the advancement of science and the arts. They were also great believers in the necessity of truth. One of Voltaire's most famous sayings is "Those

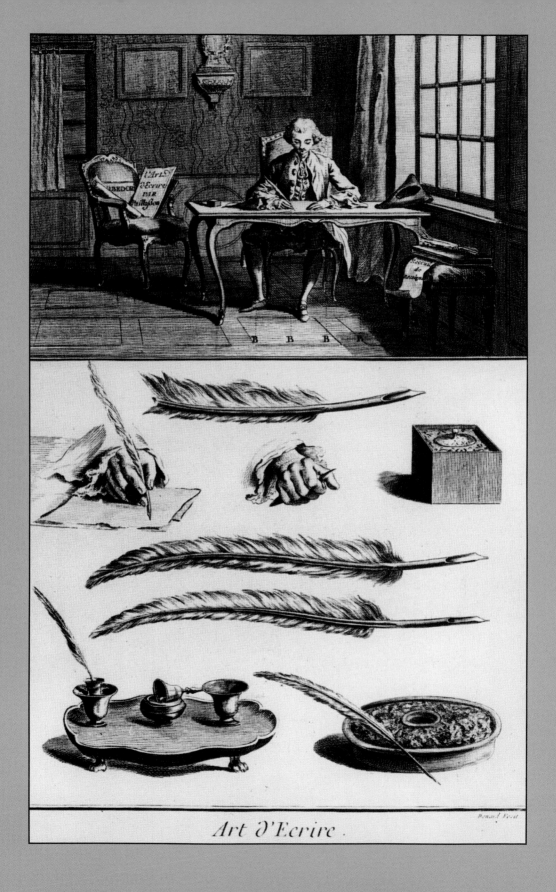

Art d'Ecrire.

who can make you believe absurdities can make you commit atrocities." Like Diderot, Voltaire believed that rational thought, science, and rigorous thinking would help sweep away centuries of religious super- stition and violence, ushering in a new age in which reason and knowledge were supreme virtues. At a time when the church's word was still widely regarded as the absolute, indisputable truth, the members of the Enlightenment constantly ran the risk of anger- ing the authorities and being jailed as heretics (deniers of the official state religion) or traitors.

Though Rousseau supported Diderot and Voltaire by writing articles about music and a piece on political economics, he disagreed with them on some very basic philosophical points. He thought that reason itself was not sufficient for humanity to advance and understand the world. He argued that a belief in God was also necessary, as was some real connection to the world of emotions and instincts that exist within all people. Rousseau also objected to the idea that humanity progressed

Entitled "The Art of Writing," this is an illustration from Denis Diderot's *Encyclopedia*. The *Encyclopedia* was the most important book of the Enlightenment. It became required reading for anyone claiming to be educated.

Diderot had already developed a reputation as a revolutionary thinker when he was hired to edit the *Encyclopedia*. His antireligious stance in *An Essay on Blindness*, published in 1749, landed him in prison for several months.

merely by adding to its list of artistic and scientific accomplishments. Simply writing more books and solving more equations was not the key to progress, he argued.

ROUSSEAU THE MUSICIAN

While Rousseau was contributing articles to the *Encyclopedia*, he was also hard at work on his own compositions. In 1752, he composed *The Village Fortune-Teller* (Le Devin du Village), an opera about a couple whose love is broken up by a meddling rich noble, but is brought back together by a humble village fortune-teller.

It was performed before the French royal court at Fontainebleau and was gloriously successful. After its performance, the king of France made overtures to Rousseau about offering him a royal pension. This

This is a page from the score of Rousseau's opera *The Village Fortune-Teller*. Despite its success, he didn't produce many others. However, he maintained a lifelong interest in this one. He revised six of its songs in the final year of his life.

stable supply of cash would have allowed Rousseau to continue composing while living a life of comfort and luxury. Rousseau, however, passed up a chance to meet the king and scoop up the pension. He explains his decision in *The Confessions*:

> I was losing, it is true, the pension which had been, in a way, offered to me; but at the same time I was freeing myself from the dependence it would have imposed upon me. Farewell truth, liberty, and courage! How should I be able ever to speak again of independence and disinterestedness? So long as I took that pension, I should have to flatter or be silent.

Unlike many of his peers, Rousseau avoided entering agreements that compromised his right to speak his mind. He seemed to revel in the chance to write declarations of freedom that infuriated the wealthy and powerful people of Europe.

This stands in direct contrast to philosophers such as Hugo Grotius, who wrote philosophy in defense of the power of kings. Rousseau comments on Grotius in *The Social Contract*:

> Grotius, a refugee in France, discontented with his own country and out to pay court

to [King] Louis XIII [of France], to whom his book is dedicated, spares no pains to rob peoples of all their rights and to invest those rights, by every conceivable artifice, in kings . . . [But] the truth brings no man a fortune; and it is not the people who hand out embassies, professorships, and pensions.

Hugo Grotius was a leading Dutch diplomat, lawyer, and philosopher of the seventeenth century. His 1625 treatise *On the Law of War and Peace* was one of the first major contributions to modern international law. For this reason, he is widely known as the father of international law.

In 1753, Rousseau wrote one of the most immediately controversial documents of his lifetime: "The Letter on French Music" (Lettre sur la Musique Françoise). In it, he suggested that Italian was a language better suited than French to singing opera.

By the time the letter had made its rounds, enraged Frenchmen had burned effigies—dummies meant to symbolize someone—of Rousseau.

According to his *Confessions*, the letter was so offensive to so many people that it had stopped a political uprising by uniting all the squabbling groups in France against his musical criticism.

Because of the way it challenged established French society, "The Letter on French Music" was the one creation of Rousseau's that met the universal approval of his compatriots at the *Encyclopedia*. They were almost always inclined to support rebels who challenged established society.

Two
DISCOURSES

CHAPTER 3

Three years before his opera burst onto the European music scene, Rousseau made an equally big splash in the world of philosophy by publishing an essay about the arts and sciences.

Encouraged by his friend Diderot, Rousseau entered a prestigious contest sponsored by the Academy of Dijon, a scholars group similar to a modern university. Contestants were required to write an essay answering the question, "Has the progress of the arts and sciences contributed to the purification or the corruption of morals?" In other words, they were to explore whether people become wiser and more gentle toward each other, or crueler and more foolish, when women and men make scientific discoveries, create artwork such as paintings or symphonies, and generally discover new things about the world.

Rousseau's philosopher friends largely had a simple answer to the question: progress in the arts and sciences made humankind stronger, smarter, more compassionate, more educated, and more modern.

Despite his own personal accomplishments as a composer of music and writer of philosophy, Rousseau felt deeply and passionately different. He broke with his friends and took a radical new stance in his *Discourse on the Sciences and the Arts* (Discours sur les sciences et les arts), published in 1750.

Instead of sticking up for the arts and sciences that he and his friends spent so much time practicing, critiquing, and celebrating, Rousseau condemned them for weakening society. He used the example of China—which was conquered in the thirteenth century by the Mongolian ruler Genghis Khan—as a persuasive piece of evidence that learning alone did not make a society great. He wrote:

> If the sciences really bettered manners, if they taught man to spill his blood for his country, if they heightened his courage; the inhabitants of China ought to be wise, free, and invincible.

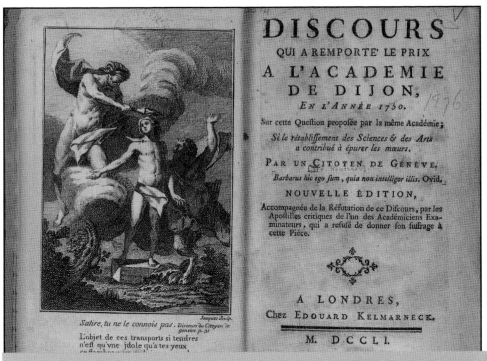

This is the title page from a 1751 publication of Rousseau's *Discourse on the Sciences and the Arts*. Although this controversial winner of the Academy of Dijon essay contest upset some of Rousseau's friends and colleagues, it established him as one of the most consequential thinkers of the day.

But if they are tainted with every vice, familiar with every crime; if neither the skill of their magistrates, nor the pretended wisdom of their laws, nor the vast multitude of people inhabiting that great extent of empire, could protect or defend them from the yoke of an ignorant Barbarian Tartar, of what use was all their art, all their skill, all their learning?

Rousseau's essay was a slap in the face to his friends at the *Encyclopedia*. He had worked side by

This painting by Michel François Dandre-Bardon portrays an eighteenth-century literary salon. Salons were crucial to the Enlightenment, as they provided the best opportunities for networking and sharing ideas among philosophers, scientists, musicians, and artists. They were typically hosted by rich women who rarely joined in the intellectual discussions.

side with them to create a work of writing that was a collection of the best that the arts and sciences had to offer, and had then written an essay that directly attacked their work and their philosophy.

He won the Academy of Dijon's contest with his daring words, however, and the *Discourse on the Sciences and the Arts* helped cement his reputation as a serious thinker on the rise.

His first major discourse signaled themes that would recur throughout Rousseau's later work. Rousseau deeply believed that there was more to life than science and rational thought, and that certain truths—such as the existence of God, the need for individual freedom, and the value of all life—outweighed whatever philosophers and writers might come up with.

His *Discourse on the Sciences and the Arts* made the case that real goodness was possible only in simple societies that lived frugally. Modern, sophisticated culture, he suggested, was a recipe for corruption, weakness, and unhappiness. This theme would be much more fully developed within his second discourse. Entitled *A Discourse on the Origin and Foundations of Inequality Among Mankind* (Discours sur l'Origine et Les Fondemens de l'Inegalité Parmi les Hommes), it is more widely referred to as *A Discourse on Inequality*. It is one of the books most responsible for Rousseau's lasting fame and influence.

Diderot, both cheerful and tolerant, found Rousseau's argument to be amusing and intellectually challenging. But it was an open break with his comrades among Paris's up-and-coming thinkers and was a sign of many more things yet to come.

A DISCOURSE ON INEQUALITY

Rousseau completed *A Discourse on Inequality* in 1755, in response to another question posed by the

Academy of Dijon. The question was straightforward but challenging to answer: why is there inequality among men?

Rousseau's paper did not win the prize. However, it had a significant impact on Western thought in the centuries to come.

The paper, as a whole, is a kind of fable (a fictional story that contains a lesson) about the development of humanity as a whole. Written as an account of the lives of the first human beings, it doesn't draw its descriptions from evidence the way modern anthropologists might do when writing accounts of how our distant ancestors lived and evolved. Rousseau wrote that he would deal with the facts "by setting them aside." Instead, it is a carefully spun philosophical story in which Rousseau imagines what life for the first humans might have been like, and then draws conclusions about modern life based on his insights about these early men and women.

EARLY HUMANS VERSUS MODERN SOCIETY

In Rousseau's opinion, early men and women lived relatively uncomplicated and harmonious lives. People largely kept to themselves. Without property or even large communities, problems such as wars,

This engraving, *Tithes, Taxes, and Graft*, depicts the crushing burden on the peasantry by the clergy and the nobility. Peasants were subject to heavy taxes, which they owed to the king, the church, and their landlords. These taxes, plus the general social order, kept most of them in a hopeless cycle of poverty. According to Rousseau, such inequality and oppression were a result of modern society.

theft, and jealousy didn't exist. Violence was rare, and when it did occur, it was quickly over. Long feuds and complicated cycles of revenge didn't exist in a time when there weren't long-standing ties between individuals.

Rousseau's early people had lives that lacked deep moral reasoning—the ability to understand the difference between right and wrong—but they were essentially content. The size of the human race was balanced by the amount of resources available, and even illness was not a serious problem. Like animals, sick humans would either recover quickly or die, thus freeing up food, water, and shelter for other people. Either way, suffering was short.

In addition, the differences between individual women and men were all real and natural. Certainly some people were stronger, smarter, or more agile than others. But the difference between natural attributes, according to Rousseau, was a fair reason for some people to succeed more than others.

By contrast, in modern society, the differences between people that really matter are artificial—created by the opinions of women and men, not natural differences, according to Rousseau. Some people are richer than others, and they are, therefore, more favored by their fellow humans. Some have more distinguished parents or grandparents, and their famous family names protect them and put them on a higher level than other people. Some come from races or religions that are more established and more popular in some places than in others.

Rousseau also thought that the advent of society created unnatural divisions between men and women, giving women too much power over men by letting them use romantic love as a leash. He writes:

> Now it is easy to see that the moral part of
> love is an artificial sentiment, born of usage

in society, and cultivated by women with much skill and care in order to establish their empire over men, and so make dominant the sex that ought to obey.

In other words, Rousseau argued that many of the modern world's biggest problems can be traced to differences that did not emerge until society, sophisticated language, and generations of tradition created them. Natural inequalities, argued Rousseau, were magnified and made permanent by the appearance of civilization. The existence of money and property, far from making people happier, actually made them miserable.

In addition, Rousseau argued that natural humans are free in three ways that are altered or violated by complicated modern society. First, early people, like animals, had only to worry about following their instinct. No complicated moral decisions were required, and no artificially dangerous social interactions existed to be figured out. People simply did what came naturally. Second, early people were politically independent, as they were completely free of any kind of government. This anarchic freedom meant that no kind of tyranny could compromise their essential freedom and rights. Finally, early people were blessed with personal freedom. Without bosses, masters, or social superiors, people did not have to answer to other people's whims and orders. There was no economic exploitation to contend with, and no workhouses or factories to be shackled to by the need for a paycheck.

QUESTIONING HOBBES

Rousseau's concept of early humans—and the "state of nature" in which they existed—collided head on with the ideas of Thomas Hobbes (1588–1679), the highly esteemed British philosopher. Rousseau thought that human beings had no interest whatsoever in leaving the state of nature. Hobbes thought they had every reason in the world to enter the modern age, forming governments and communities.

Hobbes had famously written that life in a state of nature was "solitary, poor, nasty, brutish, and short." It was a war of all against all, kill or be killed, a chaotic and horrible time for humankind. Far from existing in a peaceful, sustainable way, men and women lived in terror and squalid conditions that were horrible and best eradicated by any form of government possible. Nothing could be less desirable than the total anarchy of living without social restraints.

For Hobbes, men and women were not naturally good, as Rousseau wrote in *A Discourse on Inequality*; they were selfish and, left to their own devices, would tear one another apart. A social contract of some sort—an agreement that a society keeps among its members—is required to ensure that people look out for the good of other people, instead of simply brutally exploiting or killing them whenever possible.

England's Thomas Hobbes was a major philosopher of the seventeenth century. His writings were of considerable interest to the Enlightenment thinkers, who largely rejected his view of human nature while embracing the basic idea behind his theory of a social contract between rulers and the general population.

Rousseau passionately disagreed. Early men and women, he argued, were motivated primarily by two very important emotions that tempered the harsh conditions and made life in early times both tolerable and, in some ways, even desirable.

The first was *amour de soi*, or "self-preservation," which was a kind of self-regard. It led people to take care of their own needs and ensure their own safety, but it wasn't vanity or destructive selfishness. Rousseau argued that after the emergence of modern society, this pure emotion became something called *amour-propre*, or "pride." This was a desire to be superior to others, and to be admired by them. He viewed this as one of the main downfalls of civilized society.

The second emotion that moderated Rousseau's state of nature was *pitié*, or compassion. It was an emotion of empathy that even animals feel about members of their own species—a compassion that leads animals to avoid killing their fellows unless absolutely necessary. Horses, writes Rousseau, avoid trampling living creatures whenever possible. Cows lie down upon entering a slaughterhouse; they're saddened by death, just as we are. *Pitié*, he suggests, is something all thinking animals have in common.

Rousseau agreed that there comes a time in human history when it's person against person, and the weak is crushed under the heels of the strong. But for him, that time was not during the state of nature—before the emergence of government or complicated communities—as Hobbes argued. It was only after the introduction of property, for example, that people began to truly hoard food and exploit the labor of other people. Those who had land enjoyed more power than those who did not. Landowners would team up with other landowners who shared common interests in order to fight rivals. Writing in the second section of his essay, Rousseau states:

> The first man who, having enclosed a piece of land, thought of saying "This is mine" and found people simple enough to believe him, was the true founder of civil society. How many crimes, war, murders; how much misery and horror the human race would have been spared if someone had pulled up the stakes and filled in the ditch and cried out to his fellow men: "Beware of listening to this impostor. You are lost if you forget that the fruits of the earth belong to everyone, and that the earth itself belongs to no one!"

Further exploring the advantages of having no property or valuable possessions, Rousseau asks, "What sort of chains of dependence could exist among men who possess nothing?"

Rousseau's repeated and deeply reasoned attacks on private property have led many to view him as an inspiration for Socialism and Communism. These modern political philosophies seek to control and restrict the kind of property and wealth that private individuals can control.

ROUSSEAU'S TIMELINE

One of the most sophisticated aspects of *A Discourse on Inequality* is Rousseau's timeline for the development of man. The book is seen by many as one of the founding texts in the field of anthropology, the study of humanity's evolution and development. It also influenced Charles Darwin, the scientist and philosopher whose theory of evolution demonstrates that modern mankind developed incrementally, over time, from more primitive apelike ancestors.

Rousseau's timeline is very simple and lacking in evidence compared to modern anthropological studies of humanity's development. But it makes a great deal of logical sense as a way to think about how human behavior changed over time.

First, he argued, human beings merely existed and foraged without any technology or real need to socialize. Then, they took advantage of natural weapons, such as rocks and sticks. Next came the development of simple technology, including bows and flint for making fire. Abstract comparative thought, the ability to remember and compare objects and people not actually present, evolved. Soon thereafter, people began to be able to feel inferior or superior to—and part of a community with—other people.

With the development of larger communities, more complicated toolmaking became possible, along with simple huts. Families started to live together for extended periods of time, instead of just abandoning children shortly after they could forage for themselves. At this point, according to Rousseau, women began to become domestic, cooking and taking care of the huts in which they and their mates lived.

Language became increasingly sophisticated. With it came abstract qualities such as beauty. Love, jealousy, and violence all became increasingly part of society. Vanity, competition, and insults started to cause fights among the early men and women.

Then came the two big steps forward. The first was agriculture, the practice of farming crops on a large scale and on an organized schedule. The second was what Rousseau called "the deadly secret," metallurgy. The mining, refining, and shaping of metal allowed for a quantum leap forward in the complexity of tools; the deadliness of weapons; and the beauty of arts and crafts objects, such as jewelry and mirrors.

At this point, humanity truly stepped out of the state of nature into a modern world where people planned events far in advance, property and class divided people into different groups, and most of the instinct-driven freedom that all people once enjoyed had been completely lost.

THE TRAGEDY OF THE COMMONS

Rousseau described how the end of the state of nature set up a situation where humans went from being solitary and independent to being actively competitive. Farmers, for example, developed an interest in having many children. Children were cheap labor and a kind of old-age insurance. Having many children meant having many young workers to take care of aging parents.

Moreover, life was a dangerous prospect in a world before modern medicine. Children quite often died from disease and other causes, and if a farmer's wife gave birth to ten kids, he might be considered lucky if five of them lived to see their teenage years.

However, the more children farmers had, the more the overall well-being of the community went down, as resources such as water and land become increasingly scarce. Therefore, when an individual improved her or his own situation, the whole community suffered and declined.

One of the most common ways to describe this situation is to imagine a group of farmers who

Entitled *The Haycart*, this 1641 painting by Louis Le Nain shows peasant families at home. Peasants typically worked on the farms where they lived, and children were put to work on the land as soon as they were able to. Very small children had light chores. However, by age eight, young boys would begin to learn the work of their fathers. In addition to their chores on the farm, young girls were taught how to cook, weave cloth, grow vegetables, and perform the duties of a good wife and mother.

share a patch of land. The land is used to feed their cattle. Each farmer has an interest in acquiring more cows and allowing them to feed from the common land, known as the commons. But after a certain number of cows have been added, the land's capacity to grow grass runs out. All the cows start to go hungry and everyone is worse off than before, despite having added many cows to their personal flocks.

COLONIES OF "NOBLE SAVAGES"

The idea of the noble savage led many European explorers to take a well-meaning but often dehumanizing view of the less-developed people they would encounter while traveling remote parts of Africa and Asia. Rather than viewing the native peoples they encountered as full human beings with all the complexity, intelligence, and emotions of Europeans, they regarded them as almost another kind of creature altogether.

The simple natives, argued European conquerors, could not fully understand modern society, and, therefore, didn't deserve the same political or economic rights as European colonists and soldiers.

THE "NOBLE SAVAGE"

The term "noble savage" first occurred in a work written by British author John Dryden in 1672. However, it wasn't until Rousseau's *Discourse on Inequality* that it truly became a fully developed idea.

Some reading Rousseau in later years have seen his second discourse as a statement in favor of the

AUX GRANDS HOMMES LA PATRIE RECONNOISSANTE.

Le Génie de VOLTAIRE et de ROUSSEAU Conduisit ces ecrivains Célebres au temple de la gloire & de l'Immortalité.

VOLTAIRE (François Marie Arouet de) né à Chateney prés de Paris le 20 Fevrier 1694. mort à Paris le 30 Mai 1778. âgé de 84 ans 3 mois et quelques jours.
ROUSSEAU (Jean Jacques) né à Geneve le 28 Juin 1712. mort à Ermenonville le 2 Juillet 1778. âgé de 66 ans et quelques jours.

This early nineteenth-century engraving captures the esteem for Rousseau and Voltaire among the French. The inscription at the bottom reads "The genius of Voltaire and Rousseau led these famous writers to the temple of glory and immortality." These two giants of the Enlightenment began as friends but grew to hate each other.

goodness and purity of primitive people, arguing, in effect, that they are better than modern people.

What Rousseau actually argues is that the so-called noble savage existed in a much simpler world that lacked any concept of vice and virtue, or "good" and "evil." People in the state of nature weren't better than modern men and women; they just existed in a much simpler world that lacked the same kinds of moral judgments and complications that we face today. They did what they needed to in order to survive, whatever that might be, and they avoided taking life unless it was necessary for survival.

Voltaire, who was critical of much of Rousseau's philosophy, criticized Rousseau's ideas on humanity in the state of nature quite bitterly. "No one has employed so much intelligence to turn us men into beasts," he would write about *A Discourse on Inequality*. Although somewhat flattering to Rousseau, it was not a positive review of his ideas.

Regardless, the idea of the noble savage would have much influence on art and literature in the years to come. Mary Shelley's *Frankenstein*, published in 1818, is one example; the simple, instinct-driven monster has many of the idealized attributes of Rousseau's presocial men and women. The science-fiction writer Aldous Huxley, whose works are full of sophisticated political and philosophical concepts, drew on the noble savage concept in his famous 1932 novel *Brave New World*. Also, the German writer Karl May used the idea in his Wild West stories.

THE SOCIAL CONTRACT AND *ÉMILE*

CHAPTER 4

During the mid-1750s, Rousseau began to come into real conflict with his fellow philosophers and friends in Paris. He considered a move back to Geneva, but Voltaire had moved there after being twice imprisoned in France. The idea of sharing a city with one of his fiercest critics and rivals was enough to convince him to stick around. It didn't help that Voltaire, according to Rousseau, was likely to corrupt his countrymen with his wily and sophisticated ways, thereby turning his home city into another Paris or Venice, increasingly filled with actors and arrogant writers of literature.

In 1756, Rousseau moved to a retreat near Paris, called L'Ermitage. It was offered to him by one of Diderot's friends. Here, and at another, later

L'Ermitage was the home of Madame Louise d'Epinay, a leading salon hostess and Rousseau's lover. During his stay there, Rousseau received many visitors and worked on his novel *Julie: or, The New Heloise*. Madame d'Epinay eventually asked him to leave after he declared his love for her sister-in-law.

retreat known as Montlouis, he was able to settle down and get to work. By 1758, he had severed most contacts with his old crew of Paris philosophers and begun work in earnest on two of his greatest works: *Émile* and *The Social Contract*. Both would be published in 1762, igniting a firestorm of controversy that drove Rousseau from France.

THE SOCIAL CONTRACT

The Social Contract was, in many ways, a counterpart and an answer to the criticism of *A Discourse on*

Inequality. In it, Rousseau suggested that human instinct alone was insufficient for a healthy, free, moral society. He wrote that he had found that "the mere impulse of appetite is slavery, while obedience to a law which we prescribe to ourselves is liberty."

The discourse suggested that humanity had fallen from a state of grace when it developed a complicated, modern way of living. Also, it argued that the essential freedoms of men and women had been compromised by unnatural inequalities and the pressure of property and complicated communal relationships.

The Social Contract looked at the modern mess and suggested a way out: an agreement between people that would bring them together in some form of mutual harmony, instead of driving them apart and making them miserable.

Unlike Hobbes, who suggested that any kind of association was better than the chaos and horror of the state of nature, Rousseau argued that human freedom was not something that could be surrendered to kings or slave owners. It was something sacred and inalienable. *The Social Contract*, therefore, was Rousseau's way of addressing a crucial and ultimately unanswerable question: what form of government preserves human freedom and provides political authority that is truly legitimate?

DU
CONTRACT SOCIAL;
OU
PRINCIPES
DU
DROIT POLITIQUE.

Par J. J. ROUSSEAU,
Citoyen de Geneve.

—— *foederis æquas*
Decamus leges.　　　ÆNEID. XI.

A AMSTERDAM,
Chez MARC MICHEL REY.
M DCC LXII.

In other words, might does not make right. Brute strength and violence, in Rousseau's opinion, are not enough to make a legitimate government, even if all its opponents are intimidated or killed, and it can use its power to assure law and order. There must be some sort of mandate from the people, carefully monitored and constantly renewed, for a government to be truly valid.

For Rousseau, politics and morality were critically linked. Unlike other philosophers who suggested that the only thing a government needed to rule was power, Rousseau demanded that governments have a legitimate anchor in the people as a whole.

Only the people as a whole, argued Rousseau, had sovereignty, or the right to create laws and have the final say over decisions that affect everyone in society. Therefore, the only legitimate government was a government of the people and by the people, constantly voting to make sure that the general good is upheld.

This is the title page of *The Social Contract*, in which Rousseau outlined his thoughts on political institutions. His ideas of government of the people were not well received by France's political and religious authorities. The book was banned by decree shortly after its publication, and copies were returned to the printing house in Amsterdam.

Chaine d'esclaves venant de l'intérieure.

Like other Enlightenment philosophers, Rousseau was critical of slavery. He discusses the issue in the early chapters of *The Social Contract*, arguing that slavery is against nature. France traded and used African slaves throughout its colonies during much of the seventeenth and eighteenth centuries. This 1814 engraving portrays a group of slaves being led to the West African coast by traders.

People can't give their power away to a king, slaveholder, or dictator, Rousseau argued. Their sovereignty and freedom were inalienable and meant to be enforced only by their elected representatives.

In *The Social Contract*, after describing why war crimes are immoral, Rousseau directly attacks an old justification for slavery that was still widely accepted during his lifetime. It stated that slavery is a deal made between slave and owner, where the slave trades away his or her freedom in return for having his or her life spared. Rousseau argues that just as it is wrong for a country to slaughter the civilians or captured soldiers of another country it has been at war with, it is also wrong to force other men and women into slavery. He writes:

> If war gives the conqueror no right to massacre a conquered people, no such right can be invoked to justify their enslavement. Men have the right to kill their enemies only when they cannot enslave them, so the right of enslaving cannot be derived from the right to kill. It would there be an iniquitous [unfair] barter to make the vanquished purchase with their liberty the lives over which the victor has no legitimate claim.

Rousseau later concludes:

> The words "slavery" and "right" are contradictory. They cancel each other out. Whether as between one man and another, or between one man and a whole people, it would be absurd to say: "I hereby make a covenant [deal] with you which is wholly at your expense and wholly to my advantage;

I will respect it so long as I please and you shall respect it so long as I wish."

Thus, Rousseau says, it's ridiculous to argue as Grotius does that a free people can choose to give themselves to a king.

This opens the door for proposing a new form of government that recognizes the freedom of all people. In an effort to do so, *The Social Contract* captures many of the facets of Genevan government—and Rousseau's idealized vision of what ancient Greek and especially ancient Roman governments were like—and combines them into a proposal for a new, visionary way that people can master their own destinies.

Family ties or brute force, argued Rousseau, were not enough to make a legitimate government. The revolutionary aspect of *The Social Contract* was its suggestion that political power had to be derived from the people, who were the ultimate masters of their own destiny. Rousseau's new government had one key goal: to serve the general will.

THE GENERAL WILL

One of the most critical yet difficult to define ideas within *The Social Contract* is that government must serve the interests of not simply the majority of people, or a chosen few, but the good of the community as a whole. That collective good, or the healthy interests of the whole community, was referred to as "the general will."

Rousseau made three clear statements about the general will. First, that it doesn't have to be unanimous. Thus, some people can disagree with it, and it still remains valid. It is critical, however, that all votes be counted on all decisions. Second, the general will can never be corrupted, but it can be misled. We always want what is good, but we can't necessarily tell what that is. Finally, the general will is not "the will of all," or a simple sum of all the individual desires added up. Instead, it follows the communal interest—what is good for the group of people as a whole, not the desires of a single large group or a small group of powerful individuals.

Therefore, the general will is to be served by a government that is empowered by the sovereignty of the people. That sovereignty, in turn, is inalienable (cannot be given away or stolen), indivisible, absolute, and sacred.

Rousseau deliberately left a lot of the specifics out, knowing that his plan was idealistic (impossible to implement perfectly) and necessarily general. He suggested that the specifics would depend on the customs and people of whatever country tried to implement his ideas.

However, there was at least one clear, dangerous contradiction even in this general, idealistic plan for government. If government is serving one unified grand plan, and it is empowered by the people as a whole, who have perfect, indivisible power, how can anyone object to what the government chooses to do, except by voting? In other words, how could the government be challenged without it being seen as an attack on the sacred "people" as a whole?

In many senses, such a challenge was impossible. If an individual challenges the general will, writes Rousseau, "This means nothing less than that he will be forced to be free." Although some have argued that this passage is aimed at lawbreakers such as robbers and murderers, who need to be imprisoned for the good of the general will, others may read it as an endorsement of a totalitarian, or absolute, government that allows no serious dissent. In this light, Rousseau's government, empowered to represent the perfect interests of all people, could justify many kinds of horrible actions that would be—at least on the surface—in the "general will," and therefore impossible to argue against.

Rousseau's practical vision, based as it was on a smaller city like Geneva, seems to be for government directly for and by the people to take place in areas where all people could be involved in some kind of direct democracy. It envisioned all citizens taking some kind of personal action to guide government, like a club where all decisions are made by the votes of all members. However, when applied to a much larger country—as it was in France, during the revolution—Rousseau's *Social Contract* served as a partial blueprint for one of the most daring and violent experiments in government in human history.

DE JURE AND *DE FACTO*

Much of *The Social Contract* is spent discussing two terms that are still used in legal textbooks, international embassies, and courtrooms today. If you went to someone's house, threw them out onto the street, and then changed the lock, you would own it *de facto*, or "in fact." You occupy the house, and its former owner can't get back in. It is literally yours until someone else throws you out. If you instead bought the house from the owner in a sale that was legal, you would own the house *de jure* (legally and morally) as well as de facto.

For many political philosophers, the only concept that merits serious discussion is the idea of de facto power. If a government has power, it is, at least in some ways, legitimate, regardless of how it came by that power. An argument against this sort of thinking, counters Rousseau, is that illegitimate governments that are not overseen by the people are:

* Often thrown into chaos by crises over succession (who will rule after the current ruler has been removed)

* Subject to rule by inept people

* Vulnerable to manipulation by men of small talent and great ambition

In this way, Rousseau took a direct shot against monarchies (rule by kings or queens) that were supported by thinkers such as Hobbes and Grotius.

Rousseau sided with one of his biggest influences, Niccolò Machiavelli, who was a passionate antimonarchist and supporter of republican government. Republican governments were voted into office by the people as a whole and stood accountable to the people's votes.

Machiavelli's most famous book, *The Prince*, is a manual for how an unscrupulous monarch should best rule over his or her subjects. However, Rousseau suggests in *The Social Contract* that it had been secretly intended as a "handbook for republicans," outlining the dishonest and dangerous tactics

Niccolò Machiavelli was a controversial politician and philosopher of the late fifteenth and early sixteenth centuries. His authorship of *The Prince* cost him his political career and saddled him with a reputation as a supporter of corrupt, totalitarian government that has lasted for centuries.

a monarch needs to practice in order to maintain his or her illegitimate grip on power.

In Rousseau's opinion, a legitimate legislator, working *de jure* with the empowerment of the people, should be a moral person of outstanding brilliance, not someone working to serve his or her own interest.

Rousseau's ideal leader was supposed to be able to perceive the good of the general will and design political institutions able to guarantee and expand that good. However, despite the awesome power given to him by his popular empowerment, he was supposed to avoid using coercive (violent and/or threatening) action to get things done, relying instead on persuasion.

At the same time that Rousseau struggled to present a vision for how a government could have de jure legitimacy, he said nothing about historical states that met his tough requirements for that kind of legitimate status.

Were Rousseau's ideas impossible to transform into reality? Perhaps, but he clearly set a very high bar for what was needed to make a truly legitimate government. His ideas were so lofty that no large-scale government could embody them without corruption. In the end, what he proposed may have been impractical, but it was not therefore evil.

ROUSSEAU AND RELIGION

Rousseau was a man who took many controversial stands, but few were so annoying to his friends, and various governments, as his stance on religion. Many of his philosopher friends in Paris believed in the power of humanity rather than the power of God and had hostile relationships with religion. Unlike them, Rousseau always professed a strong belief in God. Though his religion changed with the passage of time—born a Protestant, he converted to Catholicism, and then converted back to Protestantism—his belief in God remained steady. However, unlike most European governments (and, certainly, the major churches), Rousseau also rejected the extremely stiff, traditional, and rigidly enforced beliefs that were typical of organized religions at the time.

In *The Social Contract*, Rousseau considers the best way to incorporate religion into a state. Religion of the man—that is, a personal faith not practiced through a church—dissolved allegiance to the state, he argues. He also worried that a truly Christian state—that is, a state that was humble, nonviolent, tolerant, and prone to turning the other cheek—would get torn apart by tougher, less-forgiving nations.

This illustration portrays the public burning of *The Social Contract* in Geneva in 1763. During the seventeenth and eighteenth centuries, book burnings were mostly ordered and supervised by religious censors, with backing from the Crown. The practice has a long record throughout history as being a method to suppress free speech and ideas.

However, religion of the church, he says, tends to set individuals at odds with their own best interests and any neighbors who may not believe in the same things. Priests with too much power, he argues, also had a tendency to meddle in politics. Finally, religion of the citizen—a set of beliefs dictated by the state—rigidly enforced by the government would make women and men intolerant and too ready to believe what the government had to say.

The best compromise, he argues, is to have a state-enforced religion that resembles the way religion was practiced during the Roman Empire, with an understanding that in private, most men would practice their faith according to their own ideas. The ideal state religion would make citizens love their duty without intruding upon their beliefs. Its ideas would simply be the existence of an all-powerful and all-good God, the holy nature of the social contract, and the need to tolerate all faiths, so long as they did not threaten to destroy the state.

He ultimately comes down in support of Protestantism, not surprising considering his own faith. He argues that its ability to tolerate other faiths made it uniquely well-suited to being a state religion.

Although Rousseau supported a sort of watered-down civil religion to make sure a state ran in an orderly way, he also had a genuine, personal interest in the existence of God and the personal nature of faith. He was inspired by the story and teachings of Jesus, and saw biblical roots for his belief that all men and women were basically good.

Rousseau's book *Émile* has a passage that most clearly captures the two sides of his relationship to faith. One part of the passage is a direct attack on the materialistic—or godless—beliefs of some of his fellow Enlightenment thinkers. The other part goes after what he saw as the bigotry and superstition that defined the faith of the Catholic Church.

What is even more remarkable than Rousseau's willingness to challenge authorities, whether his friends or the governments of Europe, is the parallel between his religious and political ideas. Rousseau saw all the churches of Europe as standing between himself and God, just as he saw all the governments of Europe standing between the people and their true sovereignty.

These were not necessarily popular ideas. Despite (or because of) how unpopular they were with institutions of power, they would inspire thinkers and revolutionaries across Europe and the world in years to come.

Rousseau's reflections on the nature of religion were uncensored and cast off from his pen without any apparent concern for the consequences. This is in direct contrast to Voltaire, who was much more careful about leaving France before blasting Catholicism, the state religion.

Rousseau's writings in *The Social Contract* and *Émile* kicked off a backlash. In August 1762, the archbishop of Paris issued a mandate denouncing *Émile*'s ideas after the Sorbonne, the city's most prestigious university, had officially condemned the text and the city's government had ordered it burned by the public executioner. Rousseau had seen it coming and had fled France for Geneva in anticipation of the scorching official reception of his ideas.

Rousseau had hoped that Geneva would be more tolerant than Paris, but its government burned both *Émile* and *The Social Contract* for their challenge to religion, as well as the public order. He fled again, to Yverdon, in the territory of Berne (a part of modern Switzerland), and then to Motiers in the same territory. There, villagers drove him from his house, a story that he recounts in *Confessions*:

> At midnight I heard a loud noise in the gallery which ran along the back of the house. A hail of stones thrown against the window and the door which gave on to this gallery had fallen with such a clatter that my dog, who slept in the gallery and who had begun to bark, was silent with fright and rushed into a corner, where he gnawed and scratched at the board in his endeavor to escape.
>
> I was roused by the noise, and was just about to leave my room to visit the kitchen when a stone flung by a powerful hand smashed the kitchen window, flew across the room, broke open the door of

my bedroom and fell at the foot of my bed, so that if I had been a second quicker it would have hit me in the stomach.

I concluded that the noise had been made to rouse me, and the stone thrown to catch me as I came out. I rushed into the kitchen, where I found Thérèse [his future wife], who had also got up and ran trembling towards me. We stood against the wall out of the line of the window, to avoid being hit by the stones, and to consider what we should do. For if we had run out to call for help we should have been stoned to death.

In challenging the established order of religion, Rousseau had played with fire. The consequences would chase him for the remainder of his life and echo down through history after him.

ÉMILE AND EDUCATION

Though much of the controversy over Émile stemmed from the religious ideas that Rousseau had laced it with, the book is primarily a novel about education. It tells the story of a boy named Émile who grows up and is educated in a way that

ÉMILE,

OU

DE L'ÉDUCATION.

Par J. J. ROUSSEAU,
Citoyen de Genève.

TOME QUATRIEME.

A LA HAYE,

Chez JEAN NÉAULME, Libraire.

M. DCC. LXII.

Avec Privilége de Noffeign. les Etats de Hollande
& de Weftfrife.

This is the title page from *Émile*, which outlines Rousseau's theory on education. It includes criticism of the church and religious instruction that prompted the Parisian parliament to order his arrest. A tip from a well-connected duchess gave Rousseau just enough time to flee Paris and avoid arrest.

ROUSSEAU'S FAMILY

Despite the sensitive way Rousseau considers the upbringing of children in *Émile*, his own life was not much of an example to those who wished to have a healthy, stable family.

For much of his life, he carried on a relationship with a hotel maid named Thérèse Levasseur. They started living together in 1745, married in 1768, and stayed together until his death in 1778. Over the course of their time together, she bore him five children, but in every case, he abandoned them to the

Entitled The Last Words of Jean-Jacques Rousseau (1712–78) at Ermenonville in 1778, *this colored engraving shows the philosopher at home with his wife, Thérèse Levasseur, just before he died.*

public orphanage, rather than raise and care for them.

He would later claim that he'd been too poor to care for them and that his conduct toward them had filled him with shame. But for many readers, the contrast between the thoughtfulness of *Émile* and the treatment of his own children remains one of the largest, most mysterious, and most troubling contradictions of Rousseau's life story.

Rousseau's most serious emotional connections were with women who were not his wife, whom he described as simple-minded. He had a string of significant relationships with intelligent and challenging women starting with and continuing from his relationship with Madame de Warens.

Rousseau views as a model for children everywhere. Children, he suggests, need to be freed from the tyranny of adult expectations. They need to be set loose to learn in a way that is much more natural and much less structured.

His model education included plenty of time for physical education out in nature and a much smaller emphasis on reading books. He suggests that books are not of much use for shaping young minds and that carefully preplanned situations where children learn by doing are more useful.

Émile, for example, learns to walk by walking in a field, where he falls down as often as he has to, in order to teach himself how to get back up. He will get bruised in the process, writes Rousseau, but "the well-being of freedom makes up for many wounds."

Sexual education, he suggests, should be handled by answering all questions without embarrassment, which satisfies curiosity rather than excites it. This is a radical idea in some parts of the world today, and it clearly was shocking when it was written in 1762.

In *Émile*, Rousseau argues that Locke has the concept of education all wrong. "To reason with children is the great maxim of Locke," writes Rousseau, describing the concept as not only a waste of time, but also dangerous. He cites his own miserable experiences as a tutor of uncontrollable children, remarking that the only way to make a child behave is to demand and forbid nothing whatsoever.

Rousseau doesn't argue that children are completely incapable of reason. He admits that when they're dealing with things they're immediately concerned with, they can be quite good at figuring out the ins and outs of any given situation. In his view, making children reason about their future happiness or things that don't touch them in any direct way is a waste of time.

On the question of health, Rousseau agreed with Locke that doctors should be summoned sparingly. The state of medicine in Rousseau's time was far from what it is today. There were as many quacks as professionals, and even the professionals lacked the basic knowledge of sanitation and medicine required to treat many common but potentially fatal or crippling conditions.

In fact, Rousseau took the question of medicine a step further than Locke did, arguing that a doctor should only be summoned when a patient's life is clearly in danger. Today, this is dangerous advice. But in Rousseau's time, it was almost definitely a good idea.

Though progressive and modern in many of its suggestions for the improvement of education, *Émile* is not exactly modern on the subject of how to teach women. Girls, according to Rousseau, should be educated differently from boys. They didn't need to learn about the more complicated kinds of science and would ultimately serve their most useful purpose by bearing and raising children, he writes. Émile's female counterpart, Sophie, is content to train her voice so she can sing and work on perfecting the beauty of her walk. Women are different from

Particularly among the lower classes, medical treatment in France during the seventeenth and eighteenth centuries was rooted in superstition, religious and otherwise. Many of the people claiming to be doctors were actually traveling quacks. This seventeenth-century painting is entitled *The Barber-Surgeon*, in honor of licensed barbers who doubled as surgeons, a common practice at the time.

men in terms of their character and natural interests, argues Rousseau, and they can't be expected to partake in the same education as men.

This assessment, of course, was challenged in later years by other thinkers. The philosopher Mary Wollstonecraft opposed Rousseau's division of the two genders into one capable of complicated learning (men) and one incapable (women). In her *Vindication of the Rights of Woman* in 1792, she argues that by saying women have fallen into their weaker position due to their fundamental nature, Rousseau undermines his own high-minded ideas about the nobility of humanity as a whole. In other words, Rousseau's own sexist ideas betrayed his basic ideals of believing in the goodness and nobility of humanity as a whole.

WORDS OF REVOLUTION

Rousseau's writings had two immense consequences. The first was the way he influenced the thinkers who came after him. The second was the way his words inspired and shaped the French Revolution, which transformed France near the end of the eighteenth century. As author Arthur Koestler wrote in *Darkness at Noon* in 1940, the revolution had noble ideals that were soon eclipsed by the violence with which they were pursued.

CHAPTER 5

THE FRENCH REVOLUTION

Rousseau's revolutionary calls for the overthrow of corrupt monarchies and the installation of governments loyal to the wishes of the people began to echo in the streets of Paris during the 1770s and 1780s in the writings of the *libelles*. These were writers so named because they advanced libels—scandalous, explicit, sometimes filthy charges—about government officials they wished to destroy.

The libelles became known as the *Rousseau du ruisseau* (Rousseau of the gutter), and they took up Rousseau's rejection of the culture and morality of France's upper classes. When the revolution finally came, the libelles rose from a class of underground criminals to France's new breed of journalists and censors.

Of his hero Rousseau, the pamphleteer Jacques-Pierre Brissot de Warville wrote: "I suffer myself when I read him. I enter into his suffering, and I say to myself: why was I not fortunate enough to have known him? I would have opened up my soul to him!"

Inspired greatly by Rousseau's writing, the French Revolution was one of the most important political events in history. In the name of individual freedom and liberty, a group of citizens overthrew King Louis XVI, executing him in January 1793. They set up national governing committees that were intended to serve the general will that Rousseau described in such detail in *The Social Contract*. But these committees, far from ensuring a more fair and tolerant government that worked for everyone's benefit, became dangerously violent.

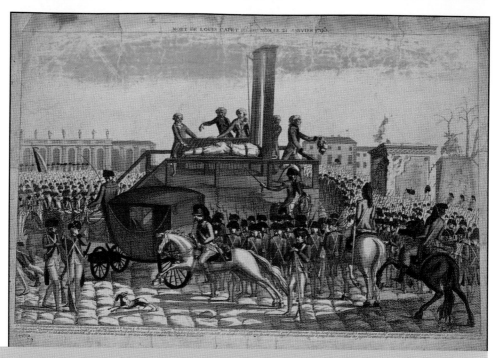

The execution of Louis XVI was a popular event of the French Revolution. Armed citizens lined the streets as they watched and cheered the two-hour-long procession that carried the king to the guillotine. In this eighteenth-century engraving, the executioner shows the king's severed head to the excited crowd.

Maximilien Robespierre, one of the key leaders of the revolution, declared that the revolutionary government was based on both virtue and terror. He said that "virtue without which terror is evil, terror without which virtue is powerless."

And terror there was. The revolution became a bloodbath that killed thousands of French citizens, many of whom were guilty of nothing more than belonging to royalist—or even moderate—political factions that were not among the elite of the revolutionaries. They, in turn, devoured one another in vicious factional infighting.

Indeed, Rousseau proposed only weak safe-guards against a government "of the people" acting violently. He argued in *The Social Contract* that there was nothing a sovereign could not rightfully do. And the French revolutionaries truly saw themselves as the true representatives of the people's general will.

Over the course of the revolution, France was rocked with changes. The revolutionaries legalized divorce, outlawed slavery, and granted citizenship to Jews. These would have been shocking developments under the reign of France's king. Although many of the changes made during the revolutionary period were seen as progressive by many French citizens, a great deal of damage was done to French society. For example, innocent people were killed and driven into exile, as a small, uncontrollable knot of people became the government of a major European power.

Rousseau's writings were inspirational to the revolutionaries, and they pointed the way toward the government they would install after the overthrow of the French king, whose rule was seen as oppressive and intolerant. As Robespierre put it: "Rousseau is the one man who, through the loftiness of his soul and the grandeur of his character, showed himself worthy of the role of teacher of mankind," as quoted in Paul Johnson's *Intellectuals*.

APOTHÉOSE DE J.J. ROUSSEAU, SA TRANSLATION AU PANTHÉON.
le 11 Octobre 1794   ou 20 Vendemaire An 3me. de la République

This engraving portrays the ceremony during which Rousseau's remains were placed in the Pantheon during the French Revolution. Rousseau's writings were tremendously popular among the revolutionaries, who saw him as a hero to their cause.

During the time of the revolution, the National Convention, a kind of revolutionary government, voted to have Rousseau's ashes moved to the Pantheon in Paris, a place of great honor. Ironically, Rousseau's ashes would be interred near those of Voltaire, his great critic and rival.

But the revolutionaries' twisted interpretation of Rousseau's ideas would have tragic consequences. By assuming that government was a perfect embodiment of the good of the people, they assumed awesome powers that were unrestrained. Soon, in an effort to fight "the enemies of the people," many opponents of the new regime were executed. Most died at the hands of a new "humane" invention, the head-severing guillotine.

Although Rousseau never advocated a tyrannical government that governed through fear and violence in the name of the people and the general will, some of his writing has been read by historians as a blueprint for exactly such a system. In *The Social Contract*, for example, Rousseau argues that factions within government are not desirable. He writes: "If the general will is to be clearly expressed, it is imperative that there should be no sectional associations in the state."

However, by eliminating parties that are formed around different points of view, Rousseau eliminated the hope of internal disagreement, which could have slowed down or even completely stopped the bloodbath of nobles, political dissidents, and apolitical (and totally innocent) people. This mass slaughter was known as the Terror.

It's not entirely fair to say that Rousseau designed the framework of the French Revolution, although his writings were central to its construction. It took creative interpretations of Rousseau's writing by a man named Emmanuel-Joseph Sieyès,

Although a member of the clergy before the French Revolution, Emmanuel-Joseph Sieyès became a leader of the revolutionaries. His pamphlet "What Is the Third Estate" was perhaps the most popular and influential piece of revolutionary propaganda. He filled many important positions in France's post-revolution government.

for example, to get around Rousseau's dislike of standing representative bodies such as committees or parliaments.

Rousseau's objection to a republican system was that the people as a whole actually enjoyed little real influence on government. He wrote in *The Social Contract* that

> the people of England regards itself as free; but it is grossly mistaken. It is free only during the election of members of Parliament. As soon as they are elected, slavery overtakes it, and it is nothing. The use it makes of the short moments of liberty it enjoys shows indeed that it deserves to lose them.

But with the writings of Sieyès as a guide, the revolutionaries were able to embrace Rousseau's spirit of popular sovereignty yet concentrate power in the hands of a relatively few people at the top of the new system. Under this system, all citizens could not act as direct participants in a democratic government.

By the time the revolution had played out, replaced by the dictatorship of General Napoléon Bonaparte, Rousseau's writings had been dragged through the mud as a template for terror and intolerant government.

ROUSSEAU AND THE AMERICAN REVOLUTION

American revolutionaries took a very different view of the philosophy of government from their peers in France. They preferred thinkers such as Hobbes and Locke to Rousseau. The American Revolution (1775–1783) was largely supportive of the idea of "negative" freedom—freedom from government interference—and traditional British institutions such as a standing parliament. Freedom meant the right of individuals to live their lives as free from bothersome taxes, searches, and other obligations to their government as possible.

The French Revolution embraced a much more "positive" freedom, the freedom to be part of a state that represented and was fully run by "the people" and provided much of what they needed, including a state religion.

American leaders rejected this idea, preferring instead a weaker state that was naturally fragmented. They had rebelled against the English king because they had grown tired of taxes and obligations to a distant, unified political system. They hungered for freedom from bonds to their government, not tighter bonds, even if they were to a government that was more influenced directly by input from average citizens.

For most of the American revolutionaries, Rousseau's idea of the "general will" was overly simplistic and not a practical way to run a government. Leaders such as James Madison instead saw government as the clashing of many diverse interests—the more interests and the fiercer the clashing, the better, to some extent. The only way to eliminate factions and differences of opinion would be to remove freedom itself; certainly possible, but a cure far worse than the disease.

Madison argued that outlawing factions, as the French revolutionaries had done, would be disastrous. "Liberty is to faction," Madison said, "what air is to fire. But it could not be less folly to abolish liberty, which is essential to political life, because it nourishes faction, than it would be to wish the annihilation of air."

According to the American system, the end product of factional squabbling was a government that reflected the many different interests of its citizens and that could flexibly respond to new, evolving challenges and interest groups.

American revolutionaries had fought a struggle of liberation against a monarch (England's King George III) and they were sympathetic to the French Revolution's overall goal of liberating its people.

Although he shared Rousseau's basic idea of government of the people, American revolutionary James Madison disagreed with many of the details of Rousseau's political philosophy. Madison, who helped to frame the American Bill of Rights, became the fourth president of the United States in 1809.

However, they saw a great deal of danger in the French Revolution's concentration of power in the hands of a central committee, and its utopian (very idealistic) vision of how government should work.

One of the great arguments of the American Revolution was about the strength of the national government. Leaders including Thomas Jefferson saw a need for states' rights and a weak federal government, while other leaders, including Alexander Hamilton, preferred a strong national government with important members elected for life.

But the French system, which cited Rousseau's ideal of a government serving a general will in order to concentrate incredible power in the hands of a central people's dictatorship, offended most of the American revolutionaries. What leaders such as

Alexander Hamilton and John Adams liked best was time-tested, practical, gradual adaptations of British government that took into consideration the basic weakness of individual human beings.

Adams went so far as to call Rousseau a "coxcomb" and a "satyr," neither of which were compliments. He had contempt for utopian theorists who relied on grand abstract systems and fancy slogans. He supported practical government based on experience, practical knowledge of human nature, and a sound understanding of political history.

The French revolutionaries were intent on carving out a brave new experiment in government; the American revolutionaries were more worried about the practical goal of creating a system that could hold together without overly oppressing its citizens or collapsing altogether.

THE HEIRS OF ROUSSEAU

Although Rousseau's influence on the French Revolution may be his most spectacular accomplishment, he also had a major impact upon the world of philosophy.

The German writer Immanuel Kant was one of the most important figures to follow in Rousseau's footsteps. Kant, who was born in 1724 and died in

Immanuel Kant is widely considered to be one of the greatest philosophers of all time. His most famous writings include 1781's *Critique of
Pure Reason* and 1788's *Critique of Practical Reason*. He described
enlightenment as "man's emergence from his self-imposed immaturity."

1804, used Rousseau's writings on human nature and freedom as a springboard for his own more formal and intricate theories of ethics. In turn, Kant's theories on ethics are some of the most influential philosophical writings in history.

In notes to his work, Kant acknowledges his debt to Rousseau, writing that "Rousseau discovered first and foremost beneath the diversity of the received forms of humanity their deeply hidden nature." He also wrote, "The thought of inequality also makes men unequal. Only the doctrine of Rousseau can make even the most learned philosopher with his knowledge an honest man and, unaided by religion, not consider himself better than the common man."

Rousseau's influence was also critical to the development of the philosopher Georg Hegel, of Germany. Hegel loved freedom and was drawn to a God manifest in nature, both ideas deeply developed within Rousseau's writing.

The English writer William Wordsworth also took great inspiration from Rousseau. In Wordsworth's writing, you can find many of Rousseau's well-known ideas. He has the same faith in the goodness of nature and children, and a similar trust in the good that people can gain from the cultivation of their senses and feelings.

In addition, Rousseau's writings had an enormous impact on the writers and artists of the Romantic period of the nineteenth century. The beginning of the Romantic period coincides with the American and the French Revolutions. This seems appropriate for a movement that intended to revolutionize the theory and practice of art, and the way people perceived the world.

Nature, love, imagination, and myth were all celebrated by the artists of the Romantic period. Rousseau's writings, which celebrated sweeping social change and the importance of individual freedom helped fuel the movement's fires of change.

The overall impact of Rousseau on politics, philosophy, and education is hard to overstate. His famous book *Julie, or the New Héloïse* (Julie, ou, la nouvelle Héloïse) was the most widely read novel of its age. His *Confessions* was one of the most influential and popular autobiographies in history. His *Reveries of the Solitary Walker* inspired

Rousseau developed an interest in botany during his later years. He is portrayed as an aged man identifying herbs near his home in Ermenonville in an engraving on the right. Below it is a page from one of Rousseau's plant scrapbooks, which includes dry plant samples, as well as the name and geographical and biological information on each plant.

a tide of Romantic writing about nature in the next century.

The Social Contract and *Émile* served as the philosophical heart and soul of the French Revolution, which in turn influenced almost every revolutionary movement that followed, including the revolutions that shaped the twentieth century.

Émile, with its carefully considered study of the development of a single boy and girl, had a great deal of influence on education and the study of education throughout the world. *A Discourse on Inequality*, which examined the development of humanity in general, inspired the discipline of anthropology.

ROUSSEAU'S TWILIGHT YEARS

After years on the run from enemies (both real and imagined), Rousseau finally settled down in his last few years, writing his memoirs (*The Confessions*) and embracing the science of botany and the comfort of nature. The study of plants, he wrote in his *Reveries of the Solitary Walker*, is the perfect subject for the unoccupied and solitary man. And solitary he was in the 1770s, largely removed from the intellectual and political communities he once had shaped with his towering personality and formidable mind.

This larger-than-life statue of Jean-Jacques Rousseau stands in honor of the great philosopher on Rousseau Island in Lake Geneva. It bears the inscription "Citizen of Geneva," in recognition of the way Rousseau often referred to himself and signed many of his works.

Comparing himself to a bear that must be kept in chains so as to not eat the peasants, Rousseau was isolated near the end of his life. He may have looked back on his life and seen a string of burned bridges, the result of clashes with other philosophers, governments, and churches alike.

Driven from Paris, driven from Geneva, fleeing from England, being alienated from the philosophers of Paris and the government of Geneva, and always living at the center of a fight or crusade or persecution, Rousseau's life had been far from easy. Moreover, many of the problems had been caused by his own combative, fearless, arrogant, selfish, and outrageous tendencies.

At the same time, Rousseau relished the last years of life. After years of struggle, he'd finally been given the chance to enjoy nature, and—accompanied by his wife, Thérèse, amid the natural beauty of France—to be free.

Jean-Jacques Rousseau died of a stroke in 1778 at Ermenonville, a town just north of Paris. His widow reported that he died "without uttering a single word."

TIMELINE

1712 Jean-Jacques Rousseau is born in Geneva, Switzerland.

1722 Rousseau's father is exiled from Geneva.

1728 Rousseau runs away from an apprenticeship and wanders Europe; he meets Madame de Warens after converting to Catholicism in Turin.

1731 Rousseau settles down in Chambery, France, with Madame de Warens.

1741 Rousseau arrives in Paris

1742 Rousseau is appointed secretary to the French ambassador in Venice.

1745 Rousseau meets his eventual wife, Thérèse Levasseur.

1749 Rousseau writes the *Discourse on the Sciences and the Arts*; it is published the following year.

1752 Rousseau's opera, *The Village Fortune-Teller*, is produced to much acclaim.

1753 "The Letter on French Music" is published.

1754 Rousseau returns to Geneva and converts back to the Protestant religion.

1755 Rousseau writes *A Discourse on Inequality.*

1761 *Julie, or the New Héloïse*, the most popular work of fiction in late eighteenth-century France, is published.

1762 *The Social Contract* and *Émile* are published; both are condemned, and copies are publicly burned in Paris and Geneva.

1763 Rousseau renounces his Genevan citizenship.

1765 Rousseau drafts a constitution for the island of Corsica and begins serious work on the *Confessions.*

1765	Rousseau's house is attacked by peasants; he flees Motiérs.
1768	After a relationship spanning more than two decades, Rousseau marries Thérèse Levasseur.
1771	Rousseau finishes an essay on the government of Poland.
1771–1773	Rousseau spends much of his time collecting and cataloging plants.
1775	The American revolution begins.
1778	Rousseau dies in Ermenonville, France.
1783	*The Confessions* is published.
1789	The French Revolution begins.

agriculture An organized system for raising livestock and/or cultivating edible plants. Along with the development of metallurgy, Rousseau viewed the advent of agriculture as one of the major reasons for the disappearance of the state of nature.

amour de soi A type of self-love (or self-regard) that Rousseau saw as typical of people living during the state of nature. This feeling ensured that they took care of their own needs, and remained healthy and alert.

amour propre An unhealthy type of self-love (or vanity) that Rousseau saw as typical of people living after the end of the state of nature.

anthropology A science that examines human societies and cultures, searching for their points of origin and how they have developed over time. Rousseau's *A Discourse on Inequality*, though not particularly scientific, is one of the first books to use a logical framework to help its readers understand how different kinds of human behavior might have began, and how humanity has changed over the passage of centuries.

state of nature A period of time in the history of humankind where people enjoyed almost complete independence. According to Rousseau's theory on the state of nature, property, war, envy, and vanity were unknown, as was any kind of complicated moral reasoning. This contrasts with the views of other philosophers, most famously Hobbes, who saw the state of nature as brutal and violent.

American Philosophical Association
University of Delaware
31 Amstel Avenue
Newark, DE 19716-4797
(302) 831-1112
Web site: http://www.apa.udel.edu/apa

Jean Jacques Rousseau Association
Carleton College
One North College Street
Northfield, MN 55057
Web site: http://www.wabash.edu/
  rousseau/rousass1.html

Museum Jean-Jacques Rousseau
Rue Jean-Jacques Rousseau 2
2112 Motiers
Switzerland
+41-03-2861-1318
Web site: http://www.neuchateltourisme.
  ch/e/museums-cities/?add_id=56&tb
  =basic&fid=30&xref=3

Philosopher's Information Center
1616 East Wooster Street, Suite 34
Bowling Green, OH 43402
(419) 353-8830
Web site: http://www.philinfo.org

WEB SITES

Due to the changing nature of Internet links, the Rosen Publishing Group, Inc., has developed an online list of Web sites related to the subject of this book. This site is updated regularly. Please use this link to access the list:

http://www.rosenlinks.com/phen/jjro

For Further Reading

Doner, Kim, and Christopher Phillips. *The Philosophers' Club.* Berkeley, CA: Tricycle Press, 2001.

Jacob, Margaret C. *The Enlightenment: A Brief History with Documents* (The Bedford Series in History and Culture). Boston, MA: Bedford/St. Martin's, 2001.

Kramnick, Isaac, ed. *The Portable Enlightenment Reader* (The Viking Portable Library). New York, NY: Penguin Books, 1995.

Weate, Jeremy. *Young Person's Guide to Philosophy.* New York, NY: DK Publishing, 1998.

White, David A. *Philosophy for Kids: 40 Fun Questions That Help You Wonder . . . About Everything!* Austin, TX: Prufrock Press, 2000.

PRIMARY SOURCES

Machiavelli, Niccolo. *The Prince.* New York, NY: Barnes and Noble, 1994.

Rousseau, Jean-Jacques. *The Confessions.* New York, NY: Penguin, 1953.

Rousseau, Jean-Jacques. *A Discourse on Inequality.* New York, NY: Penguin, 1984.

Rousseau, Jean-Jacques. *Émile.* North Clarendon, VT: Everyman, 2001.

Rousseau, Jean-Jacques. *The Social Contract.* New York, NY: Penguin, 1968.

SECONDARY SOURCES

Darnton, Robert. *The Literary Underground of the Old Regime.* Cambridge, MA: Harvard University Press, 1982.

Dunn, Susan. *Sister Revolutions: French Lightning, American Light.* New York, NY: Faber and Faber, 1999.

Levine, Andrew. *Engaging Political Philosophy, From Hobbes to Rawls.* Boston, MA: Blackwell, 2001.

Stokes, Philip. *Philosophy: 100 Essential Thinkers.* New York, NY: Enchanted Lion Books, 2003.

Wokler, Robert. *Rousseau: A Very Short Introduction.* New York, NY: Oxford University Press, 2001.

Woloch, Isser. *The New Regime.* New York, NY: W. W. Norton, 1994.

INDEX

A

Academy of Dijon, 36
  essay contest of, 31–32, 34
Academy of Sciences, 19
Adams, John, 89
Alembert, Jean Le Rond d', 22–23
American Revolution, 86–89, 92
amour de soi, 41–42
amour-propre, 42
anthropology, 44, 94

B

Bonaparte, Napoléon, 85
Burlamaqui, Jean-Jacques, 19

C

Catholic Church/Catholicism, 7,
    17, 23, 65, 67, 68
Communism, 43
Confessions, The, 13–15, 28, 30,
    92, 94
  excerpt from, 69–70

D

Darkness at Noon, 78
Darwin, Charles, 44
de facto, 61–62
de jure, 61, 64
democratic government/democracy,
    61, 85

Diderot, Denis, 22–23, 25, 31, 35, 51

Discourse on Inequality, A, 35–40, 41, 44, 48, 50, 52–53, 94
excerpt from, 38–39, 43

Discourse on the Sciences and the Arts, 32–35
excerpt from, 32–33

Dryden, John, 48

E

education, model of, 9, 70–77, 94

Émile, 52, 67, 70–77, 94
public response to, 68–69

Encyclopedia, 22, 26, 30, 33

Enlightenment, the
explanation of, 23
religion, 23, 25
science and the arts, 23, 32

F

Fatio, Pierre, 11

Frankenstein, 50

French Revolution, 9, 61, 78–85, 86, 87, 88, 92, 94

G

general will, theory of, 59–61, 64, 79, 81, 87

Geneva, Switzerland, 7, 10–15, 51, 68, 69
Council of Twenty-five of, 16
Council of Two Hundred of, 15
General Council of, 15–16
government of, 15–17, 58, 60–61, 96

George III, King, 87

Grotius, Hugo, 28, 58, 62

guillotine, 73

H

Hamilton, Alexander, 88, 89

Hegel, Georg, 91

Hobbes, Thomas, 19, 40–41, 42, 53, 62, 86

humans, theory on early, 36–40, 41, 49

Huxley, Aldous, 50

J

Jefferson, Thomas, 88

Johnson, Paul, 9, 81

Julie, or the New Héloïse, 92

K

Kant, Immanuel, 89–91

Koestler, Arthur, 78

L

"Letter on French Music," 29–30

"Letter to M. D'Alembert on the Theater," 12

Levasseur, Thérèse (wife), 72, 96

libelles, 78–79

Locke, John, 19, 74, 75, 86
Louis XIII, King, 29
Louis XVI, King, 79

M
Machiavelli, Niccolò, 62
Madison, James, 87
man, development of, 44–46
May, Karl, 50
medicine, 46, 75
monarchs/monarchies, 15,
    62, 63, 78
Montagu, Count Pierre
    François de, 20

N
National Convention, 82
nature, state of, 40, 42,
    45–46
noble savage, 48–50

P
pitié, 42
Plutarch, 12
Prince, The, 62
private property, 39, 42, 43
Protestant Church/
    Protestantism, 10, 65, 67
Pufendorf, Samuel von, 19

R
reason/rational thought,
    17, 25, 35, 38
  children and, 74–75

republican government/
    republics, 13, 16, 62, 85
Reveries of the Solitary
    Walker, 94
Robespierre, Maximilien,
    80, 81
Romantic period, 92–94
Rousseau, David
    (grandfather), 11
Rousseau, Isaac (father), 7,
    12–13
Rousseau, Jean-Jacques
  arts and sciences, ideas
    on, 25–26, 31–35
  children of, 72–73
  death of, 96
  early life, 10–21
  education, 7, 12–13, 17, 19
  family, 7, 11–12, 72–73
  Geneva and, 7, 10–15,
    16–17, 51, 68, 69, 96
  government and politics,
    ideas on, 13, 21, 25,
    39, 43, 53, 55–58,
    59–61, 62–64, 78,
    81, 83, 85, 88
  humanity, ideas on
    progress of, 25–26,
    41–42, 45–47, 53,
    77, 91
  influence of, 78, 89–94
  late life of, 94–96
  at L'Ermitage, 51–52
  modern society, ideas on,
    35, 36–40, 45–47, 49,
    53, 79
  mother of, 7, 11

musical works and
  criticism by, 22,
  26–30, 31, 32
in Paris, 19–20, 22,
  51, 96
religion and, 23, 25, 38,
  65–70
teaching and, 19, 74
in Venice, 20–21, 22
women and, 9, 73, 75
Rousseau du ruisseau, 79

S
Shelley, Mary, 50
Sieyès, Emmanuel-Joseph,
  83–85
slaves/slavery, 7, 16, 53,
  56–57, 81
social contract, definition
  of, 41
Social Contract, The, 15,
  17, 52–58, 62, 65, 68,
  69, 79, 81, 83, 94

excerpts from, 28–29,
  57–58, 85
Socialism, 43

T
Terror, the, 83

V
Village Fortune-Teller, The,
  26, 31
*Vindication of the Rights of
  Woman, The*, 76–77
Voltaire, 23–25, 50, 51, 82

W
Warens, Madame Françoise-
  Louise de, 9, 17–19, 73
Warville, Jacques-Pierre
  Brissot de, 79
Wollstonecraft, Mary, 76–77
Wordsworth, William, 91

ABOUT THE AUTHOR

James Norton graduated from the University of Wisconsin in 1999 with a degree in history. While an undergraduate, he edited the *Daily Cardinal* and founded *Flak* magazine. After graduation, he worked for the *Christian Science Monitor*, eventually serving as the paper's Middle East editor. A resident of Brooklyn, New York, he is currently the research director for *The Al Franken Show*. His experience as a political journalist and student of history led him to this study of Jean-Jacques Rousseau.

CREDITS

Cover, p. 80 Giraudon/Art Resource, NY; cover (inset), title page, p. 8 Réunion des Musées Nationaux/Art Resource, NY; p. 6 Map p. 545 from CIVILIZATION PAST & PRESENT, 10th ed. by Palmira Brummett et al. Copyright © 2003 by Addison-Wesley Educational Publishers, Inc. Reprinted by permission of Pearson Education, Inc.; p. 11 © Historical Picture Archive/Corbis; p. 13 Bibliotheque Nationale, Paris, France, Giraudon/Bridgeman Art Library; pp. 14, 54, 71 Rare Books Division, The New York Public Library, Astor, Lenox and Tilden Foundations; pp.18 (top), 29, 47, 76 Erich Lessing/Art Resource, NY; pp. 18 (bottom), 26, 49, 52, 84, 90 akg-images; p. 24 Bibliotheque des Arts Decoratifs, Paris, France/ Bridgeman Art Library; p. 27 Music Division, The New York Public Library, Astor, Lenox and Tilden Foundations; p. 33 General Research Division, The New York Public Library, Astor, Lenox and Tilden Foundations; p. 34 Louvre (Cabinet de dessins), Paris, France, Archives Charmet/Bridgeman Art Library; p. 37 Musée de la Ville de Paris, Musée Carnavalet, Paris, France, Lauros/ Giraudon/Bridgeman Art Library; p. 41 © Hulton Archive/ Getty Images; p. 56 Bibliotheque de l'Arsenal, Paris, France, Archives Charmet/Bridgeman Art Library; p. 63 Scala/Art Resource, NY; pp. 66, 82 © Mansell/Time Life Pictures/Getty Images; p. 72 Musée de la Ville de Paris, Musée Carnavalet, Paris, France/Archives Charmet/ Bridgeman Art Library; p. 88 New-York Historical Society, NY, USA/Bridgeman Art Library; p. 93 (top) © Archivo Iconografico, S.A./Corbis; p. 93 (bottom) Bibliotheque des Arts Decoratifs, Paris, France, Giraudon/Bridgeman Art Library; p. 95 © Gillian Darley/Edifice/Corbis.

Designer: Evelyn Horovicz
Editor: Wayne Anderson
Photo Researcher: Rebecca Anguin-Cohen